THE STATES AND THEIR SYMBOLS

Kansas
Facts and Symbols

by Kathleen W. Deady

Consultant:
Dave Webb
Assistant Director
Kansas Heritage Center

Hilltop Books
an imprint of Capstone Press
Mankato, Minnesota

Hilltop Books are published by Capstone Press
151 Good Counsel Drive, P.O. Box 669, Mankato, Minnesota 56002
http://www.capstone-press.com

Library of Congress Cataloging-in-Publication Data
Deady, Kathleen W.
    Kansas facts and symbols/by Kathleen W. Deady.
    p. cm.—(The states and their symbols)
    Includes bibliographical references and index.
    Summary: Presents information about the state of Kansas, its nickname, motto,
and emblems.
    ISBN 0-7368-0638-5
    1. Emblems, State—Kansas—Juvenile literature. [1. Emblems, State—Kansas.
2. Kansas.] I. Title. II. Series.
CR203.K2 D4 2001
978.1—dc21   00-022921

Editorial Credits
Karen L. Daas, editor; Linda Clavel, production designer and illustrator;
    Kimberly Danger and Heidi Schoof, photo researchers

Photo Credits
David E. Clouston, 6
GeoIMAGERY/Wesley Hitt, 16
Kent and Donna Dannen, 10
Michael C. Snell, cover
One Mile Up, Inc., 8, 10 (inset)
Robert McCaw, 14
Root Resources/Vera Bradshaw, 18
Unicorn Stock Photos/Robert E. Barber, 20; Jim Shippee, 22 (top);
    Denny Bailly, 22 (middle)
Visuals Unlimited/Roger Treadwell, 12
William Munoz, 22 (bottom)

1 2 3 4 5 6 06 05 04 03 02 01

Table of Contents

Fast Facts

Capital: Topeka is the capital of Kansas.

Largest City: Wichita is the largest city in Kansas. About 327,000 people live in Wichita.

Size: Kansas covers 82,282 square miles (213,110 square kilometers). It is the 15th largest state.

Location: Kansas is in the middle of the United States. It is one of the central plains states.

Population: 2,654,052 people live in Kansas (U.S. Census Bureau, 1999 estimate).

Statehood: On January 29, 1861, Kansas became the 34th state to join the United States.

Natural Resources: Kansas's natural resources include oil, natural gas, salt, coal, and helium. Gypsum, zinc, lead, stone, and gravel also are found in Kansas.

Manufactured Goods: Workers in Kansas make aircraft, machinery, and chemicals. They also work in telecommunications and health services.

Crops: Most of the land in Kansas is used for farming. Farmers grow wheat, corn, sorghum, and soybeans. They also raise cattle, hogs, and sheep.

The name Kansas comes from the Native American word "KaNze." The Kansas, Osage, Pawnee, and Wichita tribes called the area that is now Kansas by this name. KaNze means "people of the south wind."

Kansas has several nicknames. The state's most popular nickname is the Sunflower State. Tall yellow sunflowers grow throughout the state. The sunflower is Kansas's official state flower.

People sometimes call Kansas the Wheat State. Most years, Kansas produces more wheat than any other state in the United States.

Two of Kansas's nicknames come from its history. In the 1850s, many fights over slavery occurred in Kansas. People called the territory Bleeding Kansas because many people died in these conflicts. The Jayhawk State is another name that comes from the 1850s. People who fought in the conflicts were known as Jayhawkers.

Kansas farmers often grow more wheat than farmers in any other state in the country.

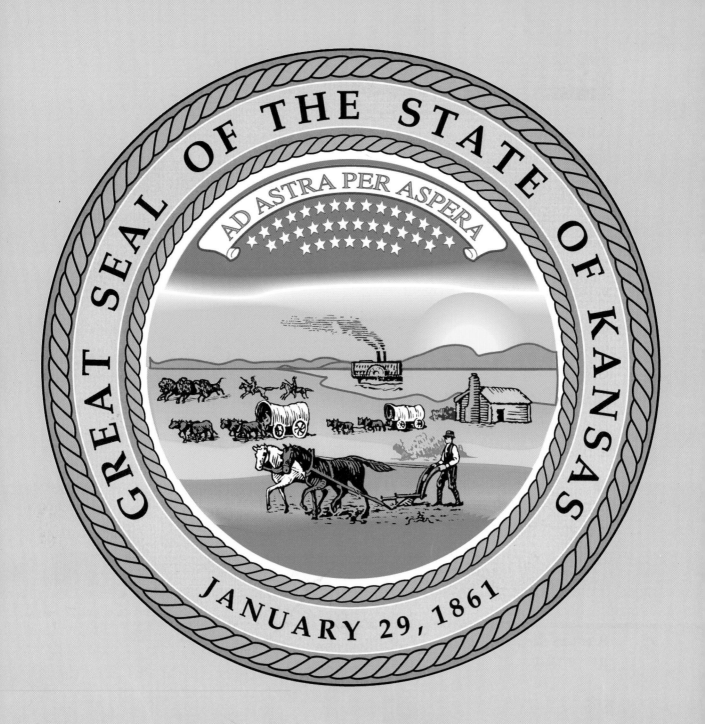

State Seal and Motto

Kansas's government adopted its state seal in 1861. The seal represents the state's government. The seal also makes state government papers official.

Thirty-four stars appear above a sunrise on Kansas's seal. Kansas was the 34th state to join the United States. The sunrise represents the people who traveled to Kansas from the east.

The seal shows several symbols of frontier life. A wagon train and American bison appear in the background. Two Native Americans on horseback hunt the bison. A settler's cabin and a man plowing a field represent farming. Agriculture still is an important industry in Kansas.

Kansas's motto, "Ad astra per aspera," appears on the state seal. These Latin words mean "To the stars through difficulties." The motto encourages Kansans to overcome trouble and be successful.

A river steamboat on the state seal stands for business in Kansas.

State Capitol and Flag

Topeka is the capital of Kansas. Kansas's capitol building is in Topeka. Government officials meet there to make the state's laws.

Workers began to build Kansas's capitol in 1866. The building has three sections that were constructed at different times. Workers completed the capitol in 1903.

A dome covers the center section of Kansas's capitol. The ceiling of the dome is 304 feet (93 meters) above the capitol floor.

Murals decorate the inside of the capitol. The paintings show Kansas's history. Kansans John Steuart Curry and Lumen Winter painted the murals.

Kansas officials adopted the state flag in 1927. The flag's background is dark blue. A sunflower appears near the top of the flag. The state seal is below the sunflower. Officials added the name Kansas to the flag in 1961.

Workers completed Kansas's capitol building in 1903.

The western meadowlark became the Kansas state bird on March 23, 1937. This songbird sounds like a flute when it sings.

The meadowlark grows to be 8 to 11 inches (20 to 28 centimeters) long. The bird's head and back feathers have brown and white streaks. These colors help the meadowlark hide in the grass. The meadowlark also has a black "V" on its bright yellow chest.

Meadowlarks build their nests in fields, meadows, and prairies. They weave grasses and plant stems into a cup-shaped nest. They sometimes cover the nest with a dome of grass.

Meadowlarks usually have two broods of young between April and August. Most female meadowlarks lay four to five eggs each time. Meadowlark eggs are white with brown and purple spots.

Meadowlarks eat grasshoppers, crickets, and beetles. They also eat seeds and grains.

State Tree

The cottonwood is the Kansas state tree. Kansas officials adopted this symbol on March 23, 1937. Many early pioneers planted cottonwood trees in Kansas.

Cottonwood trees grow taller than most trees. They can grow to be 100 feet (30 meters) tall.

A cottonwood tree trunk grows to be about 3 to 4 feet (1 to 1.2 meters) wide. The trunk is green and smooth at first. It becomes gray and rough as the tree ages. People use wood from the cottonwood to make boxes, crates, and furniture.

The cottonwood tree has shiny, light green leaves. The triangular leaves are 2 to 5 inches (5 to 13 centimeters) long.

The cottonwood gets its name from its cottonlike material that carries its seeds. People sometimes call the cottonwood the "Necklace Poplar." The seed pods look like a string of beads.

People sometimes call cottonwood trees pioneer trees. Many of Kansas's first pioneers planted cottonwood trees.

State Flower

The wild native sunflower became the state flower on March 13, 1903. Sunflowers grow on prairies throughout Kansas.

Noble Prentis may have been the first person to suggest the sunflower as a state symbol. He was a well-known Kansan writer. In 1880, he wrote, "The sunflower ought to be made the emblem of our state."

Some farmers plant sunflowers. These sunflowers grow to be 3 to 12 feet (1 to 4 meters) high. They have large yellow blossoms with dark brown centers. The flowers bloom from July to October. Some blossoms grow to be 5 inches (13 centimeters) wide.

People use sunflowers for many purposes. They cook with sunflower oil. Kansans also use this oil to make soap. Farmers feed livestock sunflower stalks. People and birds eat sunflower seeds. People also grind sunflower seeds into a grain for making bread.

Some farmers grow sunflowers in fields. Seeds cover the dark center of the sunflower's blossom.

State Animal

On March 28, 1955, the bison became Kansas's state animal. People also call the bison the American buffalo.

Bison are the largest land animals in North America. They can weigh up to 2,000 pounds (900 kilograms). Bison grow up to 6 feet (2 meters) tall at the shoulders. Adult bison are dark brown. They have black horns, a shaggy mane, and a beard.

Years ago, millions of bison roamed the plains freely. Native Americans hunted only the bison they needed. They used every part of the animal for food, clothing, weapons, or tools.

Settlers and hunters killed bison for food, hides, and sport. By 1880, less than 1,000 bison were left in North America.

In the 1900s, people worked to save the bison. Today, more than 65,000 bison live in North America.

Bison grow to be about 11 feet (3 meters) long.

More State Symbols

State Amphibian: The barred tiger salamander became the state amphibian in 1994. Second-grade students in Wichita suggested the salamander. Barred tiger salamanders live throughout Kansas. They are some of the largest land salamanders in the world.

State Insect: Kansas adopted the honey bee as the state insect on March 29, 1976. Fifth-grade students in Coffeyville suggested this insect.

State Reptile: The ornate box turtle became the state reptile on April 14, 1986. Sixth-grade students in Caldwell suggested the reptile as a state symbol. The ornate box turtle is brown and yellow like Kansas's state bird and flower.

State Song: Kansas's state song is "Home on the Range." Officials adopted the song as a symbol in 1947.

Barred tiger salamanders can grow to be 6 to 8 inches (15 to 20 centimeters) long.

Places to Visit

Kansas Cosmosphere and Space Center

The Kansas Cosmosphere and Space Center is in Hutchinson. Visitors explore the Hall of Space Museum. The museum holds the largest collection of space suits in the world. Visitors learn about stars at the Justice Planetarium.

Kansas Museum of History

The Kansas Museum of History is in Topeka. It is the largest museum in the state. Colorful exhibits tell about the history of Kansas. Several historic wagons are on display in the museum. Visitors touch, smell, and hear many exhibits in The Discovery Place.

Tallgrass Prairie National Preserve

The Tallgrass Prairie National Preserve is in the Flint Hills. A late 1800s historic ranch is at the preserve. Visitors walk through a one-room schoolhouse and an 1880 limestone house. They also follow trails through the tallgrass prairie.

Words to Know

agriculture (AG-ruh-kul-chur)—producing crops, raising livestock, and other farming activities

amphibian (am-FIB-ee-uhn)—an animal that lives in water when it is young; adult amphibians live on land.

brood (BROOD)—a family of young birds

frontier (fruhn-TIHR)—the far edge of a country where few people live

pioneer (pye-uh-NEER)—a person who explores unknown territory and settles there

reptile (REP-tile)—a cold-blooded animal that crawls across the ground on short legs

territory (TER-uh-tor-ee)—a large area of land

Read More

Fradin, Dennis. *Kansas.* From Sea to Shining Sea. Chicago: Children's Press, 1998.

Kummer, Patricia K. *Kansas.* One Nation. Mankato, Minn.: Capstone Books, 1999.

Webb, Dave. *399 Kansas Characters.* Dodge City, Kan.: Kansas Heritage Center, 1994.

Welsbacher, Anne. *Kansas.* United States. Minneapolis: Abdo & Daughters, 1998.

Useful Addresses

Kansas State Historical Society
6425 SW Sixth Avenue
Topeka, KS 66615

Kansas State Library
300 SW 10th Avenue
Room 343-N
Topeka, KS 66612

Internet Sites

50 States and Capitals
http://www.50states.com/kansas.htm
Kansas State Historical Society Kids Page
http://www.kshs.org/kids!/index.htm
Kansas State Home Page
http://www.state.ks.us

Index